CHANGE OF WEATHER

Books by W. T. Scott

COLLECTED POEMS: 1937–1962
EXILES AND FABRICATIONS (*essays*)

Winfield Townley Scott

CHANGE OF WEATHER

———•———

1964

DOUBLEDAY & COMPANY, INC., GARDEN CITY, NEW YORK

Poems in this book have appeared in the following publications: *Saturday Review; The Nation; Poetry; Rhode Island School of Design Alumni Bulletin; The Observer; The New Orlando Poetry Anthology,* Vol. 2, "The One Door" and "A Kingdom Is," Copyright © 1963 by New Orlando Publications; *The Texas Quarterly,* "The Man Who Carved Statues in Ice," "Subway Laurel," "The Tub on the Dump," "Moon-Illusion" as "Transition," Copyright © 1964 by The University of Texas; *Penny Poetry Sheet* and *Desert Review,* "That Pair—," "If All the Unplayed Pianos," Copyright © 1963, 1964 by Desert Review Press; *Fine Arts Calendar,* "To the Old Men, Not to Praise Us," "A Ledger of Sleep," "Brief Encounter," Copyright © 1963 The Little Gallery Press, Inc.; *Shenandoah,* "Postscript," Copyright © 1953 by Shenandoah; *Blue Grass,* "Amorous Out of Sleep," Copyright © 1962 by Hank Chapin; *FOCUS/Midwest,* "Rose Island," "On Re-reading the Complete Works of an Elder Poet," Copyright © 1962, 1963 by The FOCUS/Midwest Publishing Company, Inc., reprinted by permission; *Coastlines,* "—Words to the End of the World," "Four Old Boys," "S Street," Copyright © 1959 Villiers Publications Ltd.; *New Mexico Quarterly,* "The Outcast," "Master of Arts," "Unclosing Circle," Copyright © 1962 by The University of New Mexico Press; *Literary Cavalcade, A Scholastic Magazine,* "Thinking of Friends Who Are Wintering on Cape Cod," "Seneca Sprague," Copyright © 1960 by Scholastic Magazines, Inc.; *Inscape,* "Tidal River," Copyright © 1961 by Elaine Kalmar, Joe Ferguson, Jr., Ramona Martinez, and E. W. Tedlock, Jr., doing business as Inscape.

For
HERMAN
and
ELIZABETH
and
CONSTANCE
WERNER

CONTENTS

I

To the Old Men, Not to Praise Us   2
The One Door   3
The Outcast   4
The Great Man   5
The Man Who Carved Statues in Ice   6
Lost Generation   7
Peterborough   9
Penang   10
Confidential   10
Master of Arts   11
Who's Been Here Before Me?   13
On Re-reading the Complete Works of an Elder Poet   14
As in the Arts   16
Some Simple Continuities   16
A Kingdom Is   17
Dedication   18

II

Verses   20
Tidal River   21
Postscript   22
Brief Encounter   23
Verses II   23
Another Return   24

Dreamed Rain   25
The Faithless Faithful in Dreams   26
A Ledger of Sleep   27
Subway Laurel   28
That Pair—   28
The Room   29
Thinking of Friends Who Are Wintering on Cape Cod   30
A Postcard from Bedford Street   31
Habit of Years   32
The Tub on the Dump   33
Moon-Illusion   34
"—Words to the End of the World"   35

III

Ancestors   40
Unclosing Circle   40
Birthday   41
Scarlet Runner Beans   42
Christmas Asparagus   43
The Child's Morning   44
Rose Island   45
Broken Shell   46
Seneca Sprague   47
Fourth of July, Old Style   49
The Summerhouse   51
If All the Unplayed Pianos   52
Four Old Boys   53
S Street   57
For the Reason of Juana de Asbaje   59
The Transition   63

Notes   64

I

TO THE OLD MEN,
NOT TO PRAISE US

The lyf so short, the craft so long to lerne.
—Chaucer

Old men whose work is done—old artists, craftsmen—
You are liable to praise work that is like your work
And that at second hand is liable to be bad.
If we are worthy to follow you we should seem
Strange and annoying to you: not the real thing.

My generation: some swift and breathless off a bridge,
Some slowly down through many drinks. I don't know why.
Something's to be said I suppose for going still ball-quick.
Who awaits fake proofs, velvet on shoulders, medals?
And some twist in and out of madness and some
Like me don't quite do any of these deaths.

I thought this—and it is true not only in our time
But always true—I thought this on a wide-open day
In the Pecos Mountains while I stood and studied
Cottonwood leaves revolving yellow and cold
In Cow Creek among trout. I shall be old soon.

THE ONE DOOR

When you come to the door in the wall
It will do no good to knock.
First you must find the door.
It will be night, of course,
And though many times before
You have found and entered that door,
It is never easy to find.
It is never easy to enter. Wait:
Full moon and a change of weather.

Though night breathe heavy in trees,
You know what the wall encloses—
Daylight, perpetual morning,
The one place where you live.
You know but you can't remember
Whenever you rove outside.
Therefore the disturbing trouble
To find the door and enter. Wait:
Full moon and a change of weather.

There are many doors in the wall.
For you, all but yours are false.
You must rediscover the door
And then you must not knock.
Do not beat on the door.
Stand humbly, hopefully there
In what seems immutable night.
Perhaps the door will open. Wait:
Full moon and a change of weather.

THE OUTCAST

I belonged to that tribe but I never danced.
I kept the eagle feather close to my chest.
Off in the night I shook to the pounce of feet,
Dancing dancing dancing dancing together.
I shivered to the rattle of turtle shells,
To the knock of the deerhorn, to the outcry
Of ankle bells that could be instantly hushed.
I carried with me hidden the pouch of seed.
If I could not dance could I belong to that tribe?
In the darkness I watched tremendous gods
So tall they were silhouetted against the moon
That chilled the tallest, farthest mesa; I knew
Each ten-foot god masked its fill of a man.
Bird whistles and clacking of beaks. Zero.
Their tilting rush into the village dwarfed it.
They ran to bless but towered like avengers.
They moved so much like gods that they became gods.
I shook to the dancing dancing I could not follow.
Inside the masks I knew there were naked men.
Where the wind in that hollowed canyon moans
"Zuni—Zuni"; where I crept: bury me with the women.

THE GREAT MAN

That old man isolate in his mountain home:
We seldom saw him, but we knew he was there
As he had been so much longer than our lives
And—it sometimes seemed—would be forever.
Our great example. And we thought of him
Ripe with serenity of work-stocked decades
Fulfilled in unhesitant triumphs of his art
Such as the likes of us could only sigh for,
Longing for the fires on the rivers
Despite the darker winds of our middle years.

Now he is at last—and incredibly—dead,
How weigh the memoirs of the untutored woman
Who merely lived with him? That half the time
He sat in vacant-minded impotence?
Otherwise roared in baffled discontent
At what he did and all that he had done?
So she says. But what can we make of it?

THE MAN WHO CARVED
STATUES IN ICE

It had, you might say, built-in obsolescence,
Thereby contemporary American:
The statue carved in ice. A crowd of us
Assembled on a gigantic summer porch
To watch the clever man with various chisels
Transform the block of ice into a swan.
Behind him was a lawn and then the sea
And a slow lazy rain drizzling and blowing.
The clever man with fiery rapidity
Wrought a most elegant and melting swan
As though it sailed to vanish on its own river.
The perfection was momentary in the making.
Zadkine, a modern sculptor, once remarked
His statue would be good after ten years
Of birds shitting upon it in the park.
Also I thought of Michelangelo
Who cried out to his just completed *Moses*
"Speak to me!" There was a pretty girl there.

LOST GENERATION
(*Hamatreya*)

Stickney, Lodge, Phillips, Moody, Norris, Crane:
Semi-naked Apollos who farmed crocuses
In the sea light of morning on their fields,
Breezy riffle of spring flood through the lowlands.
Whatever they knew of summer, fall and winter,
They had to imagine, like the death of lust,
Like the slow evaporation of the heart
Or, as lost, the excited angers of the mind.
These men, six of a generation, loved
Their land as though it were a truth to be learned
And then a truth to be told in quickening time.
War and the memory of war: bloodstain
On green leaves where they walked, yes: never
The real red leaf nor yellow leaf nor brown.
They filed into a sudden mist of noon,
Were shadows there a moment, then vanished.
Where are these men? Asleep within their grounds
In the half-accredited sleep of young bones
Under great winters of the century.
Spring repeats their dayspring and we plough
Their furrows in fond hope of a fulfilled year
              If we are lucky
              To live it out.

              If there is wisdom
              Ever in envy
              The only wisdom
              Is to envy the old
              Grown lean and tough

And wise with work
To the final night
Of the fulfilled year.

Not the pretty crocus,
The naked foot there;
But the booted stride
In the field of wheat,
And the bundled wheat
Clutching the sun's
Mellowest yellow
Of its western slant:
This for your envy,
For your ambition,
The whole earth song.

If the old
Hide foolish hearts—
Secretly nourished;
And when dying
Call the names
Of other lost children
We never knew:
They are not betrayed,
They are winter-worn.

Luck to be spared
To live to be spare.

Leash, leash that fire.

PETERBOROUGH

I had predicted medieval ghosts
In these New Hampshire woods—and that was—
I was a boy then—thirty years ago:
Arthurian ghosts, armored, trumpeted,
Shining, riding, to circle a stone house
In memory of poems that summoned them
Out of legend alive in a dying world;
Clump and rustle of horses through the leaves
Not in Tintagel—here in Peterborough;
Among the knights that green-gowned golden queen
Whose ruin stared from every face but hers.
Then peace to everyone, dead and alive.

A boy's conceit, for love of a poet—gone
Long from here—ashes in Tilbury Town.
Again the August pause, as though the land
Had slowly ceased, as though all growing things
That made a kind of music up the air—
Opening unfolding stretching blossoming—come
To silence now by which I apprehend
How the land sang its annual emotion
Into this stillness, stillness I can hear.
Slim sound—far off—of a lark-lifted field.
A screen door slaps. Is there one summer ghost?
But peace to everyone, alive and dead.

PENANG

I

I knew a man who wanted to see Penang
Because of the sound of its name when he was a boy.
And when he was a man he went to Penang
And found it an enchanting, a Malayan, place.
He was not at all disappointed, he told me.

2

I myself, who originally came from
Plymouth, Massachusetts—where people visit—
Have once with a most definite satisfaction
Walked in the streets of Springfield, Illinois.
More than names, then? No. Nothing is more than names.

CONFIDENTIAL

In the poet's vigorous fifties,
With prolific good work done,
He writes yet more virile poems
Secretly. He hides them
To be published in his seventies.

MASTER OF ARTS

Oh, God! Just lemme have an open
drawer in which to t'row me pomes!
                    —Kenneth Lash's Prayer

Still liking poetry—although not of course this new stuff:
    "Browning
Is heady enough, my boy, if you learn to accept some idiosyn-
    crasies—
Ah, to be sure there's Frost (who isn't bad)"—
He sits in the coziest office of what is known as the Depart-
    ment of English—
Desk, soundless rug, a shelf of Oxford Dictionary, reading
    lamps, easy chair—
And confers singly with his students in what is known as
    Advanced Writing.
A bachelor with an income, thick in body and tweeds and im-
    ported tobacco,
He arranges on his desk ten Dunhill pipes direct from London,
    and listens
Patiently to the boy reading a theme aloud. And his interrup-
    tions
Are kind and accurate, for, unmentioned, he wrote—just for
    himself—when he was young
And over the years he has become a czar of the individual
    word,
Of punctuation, paragraphing, and—as it were—of the sub-
    junctive.
"Sheer?" he quotes, and gnaws at his mustache. "Sheer is a—
    a good word not to use."

The boy will remember that and the taste of winter darkening
 at the windows
But the room secure with the tidy fire that never seemed to
 need replenishing;
Though most of all the pince-nez'd tolerant twinkle which al-
 ludes
Through a most cultivated noncommittal air
To amusement at ambition in the yet undefeated undergradu-
 ate.

WHO'S BEEN HERE BEFORE ME?

Whose dictionary? I bought it secondhand
As the impersonal luggage of my language
Used heretofore, but complete, as good as new,
Unencumbered, as they say, by mortgage.

Now here, like an unsuspected meadow
Agape with frivolities of sun in a forest,
Here at page fourteen-sixty-eight and -nine,
Here between *luna cornea* and *lustless*,
This palmful of pressed flowers like a cry:
Hushed fringed gentians' faded purple hair,
Three Indian pipe, grayed-frosted miniatures,
And one embalmed-red plume of cardinal flower
Of a most blood-like, death-like delicacy.

Whose bookmarked book? Whose late summer
Pressed and dried here from the scent of light
And water-run and the shade-caring wind,
From what other year and spin of the earth?
And was it for the flowers or for the words,
The passion to hold an afternoon forever?
To fold it here—where else, lord speech, where else?—
A personal garland blessed to anonymous grace.

ON RE-READING THE COMPLETE WORKS
OF AN ELDER POET

Ways to learn to be
  More casual in the poem
    Were what I searched for:
Not—at my age—a way to write
  For I'm on to it now or never,
    Beyond even your help.
Further, I disapprove of
  Those younger men who copy
    Your three-step-down stanza.
What can they fetch but im-
  itation of personal style?
    There's no future in it for them.
Nor can I determine a norm
  For that "variable measure" save
    The beautiful ear of an old pro.
Variation—I'm all for it—
  The stain of personality—
    But each man for himself.
    That, or no real poems.

No, I was in search of
  Any way to learn to live
    More casual in the poem.
I had begun to fear I
  Slipped on a New England streak
    Of grease and gesturing wildly
Pointed morals, adorned a tale
  Or (forgive my pungency)
    Sometimes a piece of one.

Also I have been charged with
    Writing too much out of regret.
    How reply to that?
The poet must—I said—never
    Equate ceremonies of butterflies
    With those of laying cornerstones.
There is so much—even at my age—
    Still to learn: to see better and
    So to write it better.
    Most of all to stay alive.

Thanks, Bill, for all those leaves
    All those flowers all
    Those nights and mornings—
Especially those mornings and the
    Casual gesture of a magician
    With which you held
Sunlight's each momentary flash
    For good and always:
    Just for their own sakes.
Despite "the bomb"—and all that—
    One wants—like Beethoven—to
    Conclude with the human voice
    In joy.

18 October 1962

AS IN THE ARTS

Dusk overground—last light aloft in the trees—
Bird song, never since morning, lifting once more;
Then bird flight, perfected as it climbs closing,
Most effortless, the stretched wings still in the
Glide up to the bough. All the technics of evening.
Then night, and the young moon trailing a tethered star:
Familiar word, gazed at, inexplicably strange.

SOME SIMPLE CONTINUITIES

Wearied, wearied of my beggar's craft,
I turn to my children, showing them how the May
Mirror of land returns to the light
The light's praise.

Whether thrush xylophonic on the wind
Or snails' serious saraband in the pond,
Spring's wary understatement of our land
Seethes to song.

Around the ash their great-grandfather set,
The children run weightless toward memory.
Those the tree shaded have become its shade
And shade these.

A KINGDOM IS

Day, why was I summoned?
Violets, white and cold,
Shiver in the spring wind.
They are stronger than my mind
Being—what else?—beautiful.
My mind, tired and dirty,
Can hotly flail my body
Which will not stretch to answer
If it feels that white-cold wind.
My mind, tired, defeated
In endless dialogue
Of argued self-defense.
Was I my summoner?
Who's judge and jury now?
It is—I have said before—
The yellow leaf in spring grass.
Wind dwindles in rain.
Why is it difficult
To remember praise?

DEDICATION

What have we then
But clusters of images;
Tended a lifetime
They yet may fail
And fall like flowers
At a season's end.

We have to recall
It is not the particular
Bloom that matters
But rather the Idea
Of the Rose from which
All roses descend.

This becomes at last
So great a gospel
That our life's belief
Is only strengthened
As we tread petals
Withering on the earth.

II

VERSES

Sprawled with spring,
Gape-legged girls beneath boys.

Agh! why am I back to this?

In this wide
Unseasonable sun,
October noon.

Poetry poetry poetry.

TIDAL RIVER

Brindle-chick dawn but sounded by a cold cock-fall,
Morning dry with dreams. Could the just-perished stars
Sigh back my love? Grass voluptuous in the river water
Exhales a pre-dawn rain. But no rain now. A fuss of finches
Flusters the low light rising through alder tangle. A tin can
Winks in the mud, is angled to shoot the sun. Could
Clout of gull-wings, gray cousin to swan, host a thigh?
The light is a pale melt in the muddy flow, and a scythe of
    wind
Reaps an induced ripple; gone; where I lean mid-bridge
My face below is a water-troubled shadow and not mirrored,
Only an elongation of shadow while the filling river backs
    away,
Earth-colored now, from sea, and carries a dead cod and a
    stretched condom.
Opposite me, under the alders, a couple-crushed patch of grass
Makes an empty ring where night stood and that starlight
Shone steady as though it could return unchanged forever.

POSTSCRIPT

I opened to where you had written my name
On the flyleaf twenty years ago.
Nothing else—not even from whom it came;
As though you had known I would always know.

It is winter again. In the sun new snow
Stares blind white here as there that time.
How foolish I should be startled, though,
That the poems in the book haven't changed a rhyme.

You've changed, I suppose. Others do, and I'm
Two times as old as the twenty years.
To discover mirrors less sublime
Is least of griefs and which most endears.

But you—but you? One knows what one fears,
Beauty like that is not to keep;
Yet if I imagine you now through tears
It's the sun on snow, and the snow is not deep.

I have seen you only when I'm asleep,
Unchanged save the unrequited vow.
I'd have more than a written name to weep
Had I loved you then as I do now.

BRIEF ENCOUNTER

What I had never imagined: your return
In the guise of an actual girl: and there
She stood so slender in the summer light
And leaned—in such a way—the light came through
Her thin white shirt and silhouetted her
So I was shaken with remembering
And silent with impossible desire.
O I so heavy with years and all I knew,
All that she could not know—she was not you—
Yet shared (I thought) that vibrancy of silence,
Then walked to me and touched me, as if she knew
Something neither of us would ever say.

VERSES II

Amorous out of sleep, I thought:
Suppose we two should meet
After so many years:
What would our bodies do?
And tried to sleep again.

ANOTHER RETURN

Why, when we were dressed for darker weather,
Did you walk in in that slim green gown
That bared your shoulders and almost your breasts
And the young hair that way down to your shoulders?
As though you were quoting light.

Lie down. Lie down again beside me.
Was your reluctance for the others there?
Or, because you had not changed as I,
You had forgotten me and all those times?
Lie down again beside me.

DREAMED RAIN

*One looks back to one's youth as to a cup
that a mad man dying of thirst left half
tasted.*
                                    —Letter of W. B. Yeats

Woke up, wondering if I had dreamed rain.
Heard rain on the metallic palm leaves,
Wind in my window, slapping Venetian slats;
Sea and the sound of sea damped flat.
I so far from home, come south too late.

You remember those flamingos I talked about?
Years ago? That was boy talk, and I think you knew
I never really had flamingos. Only the green moon.
I was thirsty. The cup was full but I was frightened.
If you could come back now could you easter me?

I am a stranger here, so what's the season?
Cold rain falling on the long lagoons
That let salt in from the sea for all the rain.
Nobody in sight. Dark morning. All the rain
Seems not to wet alive the dusty fish.

THE FAITHLESS
FAITHFUL IN DREAMS

In dream in the second sleep,
That muscle slack on the groin
All pride of flesh drained out,
I climb dark stairs remembered
Safe from a ruined house; enter
A room of another place and time,
And the girl is there. A sea-soak of fish
Is not strange in the corner nor everywhere
A youthful taste of juniper.
How beautiful and unchanged she is
But her smile has the years along it,
Distances and refusals. I know
Unadmitted love is always known
However late, never quite uselessly;
Though perhaps not forgiven after all.
What's it to her, young, that I was young,
And we faced each other once defenselessly,
Save that she remembers. Oh, had I
Touched her, all things had touched me!
Her smile is kind but wise and older
Even than I. The moon sounds in the sea.
Grown self-conscious I shrink impotent
And those insistent stars that with the night
Build the north wall make no intersections:
Nothing can happen now, not even sleep.

A LEDGER OF SLEEP

Midnight. Rain blowing through the empty street.
He is asleep. He dreams this over and over.
He is there, waiting in the drenched lamplighted street.

He runs with melting knees toward a train
He can never catch. Never in time. Over.
He trembles at the clock lighted high. Too late.

He is still asleep and dreaming. No one
Stays long alone in dreams. Soon
He revisits lost worlds, raises the dead,
Creates affectionate girls, ravishes strangers:
Infallible dramatist of character.
Sex and fright destroy him into waking.

He remembers what Fromm taught him:
There is no "as if" in the dream.
He is tossed shaking as from a cold sea.
What friends humiliate or love him in their dreams?
Or perhaps not friends, people he hardly knows?
Suppose someone dreams him back when he is dead?

SUBWAY LAUREL

Up the subway steps they run—the boy and girl—
Surface-leap onto the summer-sun-stunned street.
Embraced and laughing they walk—and her impudent breasts—
And taut within jeans the brazen hunch of his sex.
Look—she carries a bunch of mountain laurel—
The kind you can buy out of buckets in subway stations.
Look how she carries it, torch-like, returned to the sun.

THAT PAIR—

That pair lying deep there in exhaustion
From hours of love-making: sprawled
Young nakedness, half falling away
Half clinging, on the couch in the
Silenced room in late afternoon's
Fading light: so I imagine them.

O in my wiser moments I have written
Not to look back in envy; it is waste.
Yet how not shake with jealous memory
So long as I'm still licked—briefer
Infrequent—by intercrural fire?
Perhaps some extreme quiet of old age
Will let me look at such and dryly smile:
That pair wet with sweetest wisdom.

THE ROOM

Because we were told what this room once contained—
For those few moments on that one night that fall—
We think of it, breath shortening as we stand here.
Though spring and daylight quiet a changed world.
We had known this room before as we know it now.
Whatever has happened to us, it has not changed.
And that is what, being human, we find strange.
Why we alone must alter for anguish and sorrow.
The cool placidities of chairs, walls, bed
Erect no mark at all of that naked thigh
Or the glared meeting of those opposed pairs of eyes.

THINKING OF FRIENDS WHO
ARE WINTERING ON CAPE COD

For Charles and Deborah Philbrick

I like a cold beach on a gray day. Remember
Me in November and December
When the Cape's taut arm springs bicep-bulged
Against the tides which it indulged
In the—dreamed was it?—summer of your early stay,
But now against tides ominous with spray:
How they roar in with that boom-bumbling stumbling
As if they would never halt—and no less humbling
Their hurricane-seethed screech, withdrawing;
Is there rain in your eyes or spindrift yawing
While spinnaker clouds press the far flatted sea?

When you walk the hardened dunes, remember me
As an out-of-season lover, if you will,
Where what compass grass wrote rounds stiff and still
And carved, if anything can be carved, in sand;
And amidst the cohabit odors of marshes inland
With salt gust of beach which breathes wet stones,
Dead starfish, blacked seaweed, clamshells, fishbones;
When you get, hoping for menace, that human wish
The dark day be darker before night makes its finish—
Even unseen flickers of snow, promise of storm;
And when you go indoors and begin to be warm.

A POSTCARD FROM
BEDFORD STREET

Morning in Bedford Street is
Lined with ash cans and
In most of them are stuck
Discarded Christmas trees
Bared to scraps of tinsel.
A new year.

And now at
Eight-thirty the girls
From last year's commencements
—And of course you remember—
Emerge with their impudent or
Shy walking and their
Shoulder-length hair shining
Past the ash cans and dying trees
Off to their young jobs.

And I
(Not altogether avuncular)
Imagine with male conceit
I can tell which have a man
By preoccupied, half-awake faces;
But knew only—long ago—once
For sure.

This brief return—
Old darling—to write you the snow
Melts as it used in the gutters
With its daffodil-chill smell
Under the autobiographical sun.

HABIT OF YEARS

Pointillist, the morning:
We lay late in our
Habit of years, slowly—
Hands, eyes—waking warm,
And watched the sun mount, coming
Over pillared poplars' tall brass
Thrust to new sky
Where in the windowed morning
Everything stood aged, strong—
Grass tough with fall;
Darkly flaming, the maturer flowers of fall
Lolling against stiff air:
Everything burning in a
Spiral of returning up
To the whirling suck of the sun,
Yet so close, so still; so slowly.
Then we found—
Wind-flung through the open door—
By the bedside a drift of leaves
Night-minted while we slept:
So smooth to the bare foot
As not to seem out of place
On the floor of our room.

THE TUB ON THE DUMP

Since there is nothing to prevent—not age—
Nothing to prevent my imagining
A beautiful woman stretched in it,
Moving and shining in water . . .

This tub on the dump—bare, cold, dry,
Torn out and thrown—its cast-iron sides
Ugly exposed—its enamel dull—
Here in the cloudy sun stupidly tilted
Amidst gusts of ashes and burrowing rats.
Here tin cans scintillate; the air
Breathes moldy with sodden newspapers,
Such rubbish as soiled, discarded girdles.

Dogwood her body—as has been said,
"A small flight of white birds passing";
Her body stirring, wing-shadow in water,
Somewhere, sometime, within this. A fragrance.

Great shell surfing the far shore;
O goddess naked and golden riding,
Return; whom once I knew and filled.

MOON-ILLUSION

Metastasis of sky:
Full moon again.

And moon-illusion:
What we watched so huge
New on the horizon,
Now seems a small center
At the height of night.

All is a seeming,
What large, what diminished:
A dream of our eyes.

Remember the man
Who said of full moonlight
If it happened only
Once in a century
It would be a tale
To tell to children.

Silent spread of change,
A disease of silver.
We, exalted with fright.

I have come to an age
Where I know for sure
There is no such thing
As deathless desire.
All the nerves of the body
At first dismayed
At last applaud and sigh.

"—WORDS TO THE END OF THE WORLD"

1

Never invert the tree.
O you will try in the drying seasons
And some days it can be done.
But see what is there:
Roots dying in the forced air, and all the curves of flowers
Broken and brown, head-down.
The signals of the sun are
The signals of desire—
That shuttle of light, or nothing.
Brain alone cannot say to sex, Arise.
When lust no longer ascends from the loins
Do not send for it, old man.

2

You know that terror, too:
That you are due at a place somewhere
By honor or duty, that you once knew
The way, the destination,
The expectation of you; and now the hour.
But now: where? when? how far?
Dream's dark paralysis.
Failure's dull agony.
Yet by day it is some days true
That, wondering about the unreachable place,
You turn a corner and stare,
Walk the new grass beneath the old trees.
After all, alone; yet there.

3

To begin again—
The garden
The innocence—
Is only and always to begin.
Not by mind but by flesh taken.
Nakedness thoughtless as all the curves of flowers.
And of course the girl there, too,
Not as remembered but as if new.
Unsummoned, the rose rod
By which you are driven to her
Till the world is nothing but her receiving it
There on the grass under the flowering trees.

4

But remember Koheleth.
There is a time to read *Ecclesiastes,*
When you are full-grown young,
So swollen with joy, so mad-sad,
And all so safely so
As in a play—
Yourself to enjoy yourself at one remove.
There is a time again
When you are beginning to be old.
Ecclesiastes opens the hole in the wind
Through which, soon, you will walk forever.

5

Bark-stripped, bare,
Forked chalk-white, stark, thrust high,
A tree, a white tree:
Your mark in the forest—the still wood within wind
Amid all the laving leaves of the live oaks—
Toward which you always walk.

36

Do you remember Antaeus?
Now and then you must rest on the ground.
It matters most just where
Since Earth, although your mother everywhere,
Is also at certain intervals yourself
And those not easy to discover.
You, Antaeus, are only you.
Remember Hercules, there are thousands of him
Can hoist you to death—
O aging son of Poseidon.

6

Indifferently, the sun
Nurtures and kills you.
Its golden words are two, Alpha, Omega.
Write the alphabet in a ring-round
So the two that belong together stand together:
A and Z, beginning and end, side by side.
This is the shape of the world.
God's hoop
To jump through
Once.

7

Offshore, will you watch
How the island glides toward you
As though it were rolled on the loll of bells lazy in a summer
        ocean.
Faintly, doodle of cockcrow repeats, repeats.
A woman in a doorway shakes out a white tablecloth.
All this is far, clear.
All beautiful with meaning.
Most of all the old man in the meadow
Bending down,
Planting trees above the hysteric sea.

III

ANCESTORS

Think now how it must have been in the old days:
If you could have stood (as here) above a town
In the kingdom of kerosene, in the early night,
And watched in every house, at about a time,
The ascending lights like hundreds of filaments
Curving and turning upward on all the stairways,
Each man and woman light-circled, lamp in hand,
Trailing also the slowly ascending darkness:
My God! would you not have imagined, watching there,
All round and beneath you this rise of petal-flame,
That these were torchbearing gods and goddesses
Mounting the stairs in their little houses to make
An individual darkness and to sleep, or love and sleep.

UNCLOSING CIRCLE

The old widow lying alone at midnight,
By habit—still—on her side of the bed,
Can hear across the hall murmuring talk
Of her daughter and son-in-law, also abed;
Not their words, only the sound of things said.

And she remembers how as a small child
Lying awake it was one of her mysteries,
What her father and mother abed were talking about.
Not quite closing a circle of histories,
She falls asleep down a spiral of Christmas trees.

40

BIRTHDAY

It is the time of bloom.
Here are white lilacs for you again, lady.
I inhale the swirl of years.
Do your bones live and flower?

How time comes back like water
Where foam of shadbush breaks
In May woods, and coltsfoot prints
The stone-treading brook.

It is the time that green leaves
Flicker up everywhere and pause;
Air grown tall, draped with willow,
And all our tender valleys hazed
In lace of apricot.

What begins, repeats, concludes?

Do your bones gape underground
And I thrash toward breath again?

SCARLET RUNNER BEANS

His scarlet runner beans
Climb the adobe wall
Higher than he is tall.
It is his fiftieth summer.

So far as he remembers
Their orange-flowered vine
Is his first since, at nine,
He planted some by a trellis

To be his back yard garden.
Along that seaside walk
Those must, like Jack's beanstalk,
Have towered to sky above him.

Now not so high. He observes
In the way of middle-age leisure
And lifelong torment and pleasure
The flowers are tiny snapdragon.

He resembles the man in the novel
Who never said what a thing was
But always what it was like; because
That is the way he behaved.

It is his fiftieth summer.
He smiles at his runner beans
For his knowing, once, what he means:
They are just as they were, unchanged.

CHRISTMAS ASPARAGUS

November in a dove-devoted air
Murmurous with slick whimper of wings
Across the russet caves of trees.
The pink-nosed children bring out of the wind
A tall frond of asparagus gone to seed,
Conifer-tree-shaped, most delicate plume
Branched with green thread and hung with
Tiny, most cleverly spaced, red berries.
We stand it in a jar. They stand around it.
Yes—I say—it is asparagus gone to seed
And yes—yes: Christmas is coming soon.

THE CHILD'S MORNING

Gangway for violets,
Old snow in the corner.
Sun after a rise of rain
Over cuttlebone cloud.
Sun in the brook running
Green with water cress.
Sun on the spade—
We shovel out crocuses.
Up the concrete walk
Under surf of roller skates
The hail of jacks,
Kill-click of aggies.
We summon with jump ropes
Sap in the trees,
With bat-knock of ball
And the thudding glove.
That clang of school bells
We answer with answers:
Tall immaculate silence
Of colored kites.

ROSE ISLAND

for Roderick O'Connor

Who will remember, who will know again
That isolate island in sight of the mainland?
The long cough of the rocky beach, the rusty pools
Where small crabs hustled green into darker weed?
Who will study the subterranean pockets
Tough-walled with mussels and periwinkle blue
In the flashes of light on the iodine-odored sea?
Who will know what it is in the summer noon
To stand and look back at the continental shore
As far on the harbor as if it were forever?
Who will remember how it is to kneel
By the pink and purple beach peas while the salt
Wind bends over filled with a wild-rose drench?
Or stare from the ridge at the whole island's length
Bow to stern in one embracing glance?
Who else would hear voices that are not there
Where we gazed up at tall and talking people?
On the treeless ridge in grass knee-high?
Who will know again? Who will remember
As children in the sun who loved that island?

BROKEN SHELL

My smallest and last child smashed the shell
That had been given me when I was a child:
So long, so carefully kept: a pearl shell
That filled my adult hand, its immaculate
Inner dome flushed with miniature rainbows:
A tiny cave carved in far-off seas
Whose dazzle of sun-struck gold-green
Here incredibly fixed; and the sound of seas
Which was, I grew to learn, my pulse's sound.
Now dropped and broken by that child of mine
Too young to know what he has destroyed;
Too young to tell me what I should have known.

SENECA SPRAGUE

(one for the children)

Seneca Sprague, white-bearded, old, alone,
Lived at the edge of town in a gypsy wagon
And believed in the Second Coming of George Washington.

Seneca's wagon—pitched roof, little chimney—
Stood in a field under a handy elm tree;
His horse—a white horse—grazed all year nearby.

It made a gay-looking toy house—painted yellow
With red wheels—smoke astir—as if at will
It might rock off and away like a house in a fairy tale.

Seneca hitched up only on Fourth of July.
His wagon decked out with flags and bunting array,
Early in the morning he drove it to town, down Broadway.

He parked it on the Parade, and all day long—
A patriarch of patriotism—he sat watching
Booths, bands, processions, but as if waiting for something

To happen—the event which he alone conceived
And stayed ready to receive: intense face roving
Beyond the crowd for a particular charger's hoofs

With its fatherly rider huge in blue, in gold braid,
More massive than common man, and the great sword,
The dividing crowd, the ride straight toward Seneca Sprague.

All day long he stared there over the din
Of cannon and firecrackers—and the folk who grinned
For a faith too outlandish to believe in or even to want.

In evening thick with the smoke of punk and powder
Seneca drove his wagon—it swayed smaller, smaller—
Beneath an arch of skyrockets bursting in air,

Back to the field where he furled it again to his house
Slowly and with such undoubting pride—no less—
As the prophet grown so singularly religious

Can take in annual, public testament given—
And no matter what the town thought of old Seneca Sprague.
(That was his name. This is all true. Long ago.)

FOURTH OF JULY, OLD STYLE

We say, Is it dark enough?
We are so impatient for dark.
The sawdust-odored day
Floats in a punk-smoke dusk;
All the torpedoes are spent.
Across the bluish town
Far-flung a firecracker
Singularly reports
One more echo of day.
Song of summer evening
Sings so long sustained
Through honeysuckled dusk.
The lamplighter passes
And each street corner blooms.
Now it is dark enough
For fathers to come out
To firefly-stippled lawns
And set real sparklers there.
Be careful, children, say
Mothers on the porch steps.
Then the fountains burn.
Then the fences spin
With fiery golden whirls.
Then the night curves tall
With rockets' arching climb
And over all the town
Their many-colored stars
Splinter on the sky
And dwindle slowly back
Toward damp grass and us

Though never quite to reach.
Then real stars again
The fireflies and the quiet.
Before we go to sleep
We ride velocipedes
Into the cone of evening
Down granolithic sidewalks
By July-jointed windows
Where gramophones are playing
Under the slippery elms
Into the cone of evening
Deep in the time of dark.

THE SUMMERHOUSE

That time they removed the bandstand from the Park
They must have overlooked as private property
This quainter cousin, the summerhouse. And here
It survives in a ring of elms that are sick and dying,
Settles a little sidewise in the deep August grass.

A box to let shaded weather in and out,
A frame of form, a frivolity of filigree,
Doodle of architecture, Victorian valentine,
A real but scarcely, one thinks, a serious place
Unless secretly in starlight for two lovers:
No, a midday place for white-dressed ladies
Who beneath locust-sweet and blowing airs
And a sense of not in nor out nor here nor there
Bowed above crocheting and their plans for the fall.

It would be sentimental to insist
Its woodbine, scribbled round it, loved and kept it.
It might be harder though to explain at all
How it outlasted the big house and the stables
And makes a kind of word, obsolete, whispering,
Within the incessant, cicada-singed, summer afternoon.

51

IF ALL THE UNPLAYED PIANOS

If all the unplayed pianos in America—
    The antimacassared uprights in old ladies' parlors
    In the storehouses the ones that were rented for vaudeville
    The ones where ill fame worsened and finally died
    The ones too old for Sunday School helplessly dusty
    The ones too damp at the beach and too dry in the moun-
        tains
    The ones mothers used to play on winter evenings
    The ones silenced because of the children growing away—
Resounded suddenly all together from coast to coast:
Untuned joy like a fountain jetted everywhere for a moment:
The whole nation burst to untapped, untrammeled song:
It would make—in short—a most satisfactory occasion,
A phenomenon which the scientists could never explain.

FOUR OLD BOYS

One bobolink's triplicate bubblement out of the woodside, and
    a brook's soft sound.
I spied on four men sitting in a field riffled by bluets under
    a sunned wind:
They lazed around on campstools by their tents in the field:
    four old boys away from it all,
Camping out in the Green Mountains, the White Mountains,
    the Adirondacks—
Loafing in that field of flowers; three rich men and a bearded
    old bird-watcher.
To famous and powerful men, life, liberty and the pursuit of
    happiness may
Be realized, recaptured, reaffirmed
 By crossing a meadow and straddle-legged peacefully peeing
    into a blueberry bush.

Harvey Firestone and Henry Ford, Thomas Alva Edison, John
    Burroughs, surrounded
By the field and the sun and the trees and the wind in the
    trees and a sense of Huck Finn;
They traveled in two cars accompanied by two trucks (for the
    cook, tents, lights)
Up and down and around and over the back roads of the
    world they loved and remembered,
The world that was the world before they changed it; hoping
    to find themselves unchanged.

Firestone?
He had a beautiful name and he made rubber tires, and he
    was there; he's gone now.
The others remain. Each of the three died at eighty-four:

Burroughs in a train berth hurrying home to die;
Ford by candlelight (no Mazdas), a stormy night;
Edison—how does a god die? So incredibly that we soon
   forget that he has.
But these were subsequent hours.

                    Behold this god
                    beaming above the bluets,
Hands in the pockets of his rumpled pants; five-nine to his
   pork-pie hat;
Two per cent inspiration, ninety-eight per cent perspiration; a
   quart jar of medals back at the house. The wizard's
   house.
Multitudinous voices over one wire—he would like to have
   heard Napoleon's—
"Mary had a little lamb"—what *he* thought to say at the beginning;
Cells, filaments, tungsten, carbons; faces and voices moving
   forever;
Twelve hundred patents including concrete construction and
   goldenrod rubber;
From a burning thread he illuminated the earth, now among
   the planets a brightening star.
This hardest working man in the world, this most impure of
   scientists, this triumphant tinker, this joker, this god:
Benevolent farmer of ease in a field; fuzz-browed, keen-eyed,
   deaf.

                    Whenever
One of the cars broke down on the road, the clever mechanic
   Henry stripped to his shirt-sleeve start,
Crawled under and worked his wonder. Then Edison
Strolled by the wayside gathering wild flowers. Like a school-
   boy scuffing to teacher
He brought them back to Burroughs to learn their names.

While the peace-loving and Jew-hating and wage-raising, his-
    tory-scorning Henry, her only begetter,
Lay flat on his back under his sweet Tin Lizzie and readjusted
    her parts.
In the Adirondacks, the White Mountains, the Green Moun-
    tains, the back roads
Edison loved to explore.

                  Wake-robin (jack-in-the-pulpit)
                  and bobolink
Under the cool woodside in the silent forenoon. Bearded old
    bird-watcher Burroughs—
Oom John, his friend Roosevelt (the T.R.) called him—at
    home where he was.
Friend also of Walt Whitman. A literary naturalist. Lover of
    birds and of flowers and poetry,
Despiser of woodchucks and Warren Gamaliel Harding. A
    good and a vain man.
Sometimes at townships where the old boys turned into celeb-
    rities
More folks came out to see Burroughs than Ford or Edison. So
    Oom John recorded.
He stood—he had said—amid the eternal ways; "for what is
    mine shall know my face."

Whistle me over the ridge of the sky into the valley of yes-
    terday's buttercup gold
With the sun soft and the trees dark, a puddle and paddle of
    brook water,
A living return to the earth, dreamed, to the leaves of grass,
    amid bluets, innocents' hands,
And the eyes cleansed of the cataracts of factoried years, glance
    be nimble and quick again,
Make giants to see as children see so the world grow green
    and large

In the Green Mountains, the White Mountains, the Adirondacks, wherever
Over wake-robin and under bobolink: Edison, Ford, Firestone—
It was some such song of silence they pursued—Whistle me over—inviting
Oom John, of the country they sought, a native, knowing the language, the obliterate trails.

Later, after the death of Burroughs, they took along the new President, Harding,
Who had—quote—room in his heart for all—unquote. According to the New York *Times*.
They could see he had smilingly opened America onto one big front porch, rocking away.
Not to mention the boys in the back room. But not. And Mary
Had a little lamb a little lamb a little lamb a little lamb . . . Record stuck.

S STREET

It will be seen . . .

A dark cold day, and a rain of brown-yellow leaves across the
crowd.
A small crowd in the gray street. Silent. Its faces toward the
old man on the front steps. Woodrow Wilson.
In the silence—the pause—the gust of Washington dampness
is bone-chill as a tomb.
The leaves fall methodically. There has been applause.
The pause is like the pause at a play. About to begin? No.
No, this is rather
The second before—the audience not quite certain in memory—
"Isn't it now?"—
The famous monologue. The more confident anticipating si-
lently *To be or not to be*
While the great tortured man stands staring there in his black
cape alone.

But no, he does not stand alone. Half a pace behind him a
Negro servant
Supports Wilson at his withered arm. (The Kaiser was born
with a withered arm, but this is different. Struck.)
Under the smart silk hat the tragic face is a twisted mask—
save the eyes and the jaw.
So he waits for a moment as though for himself, his spared
hand on his cane, heavily.
The ex-President of the world.

                    (Harding was already dead: as Alice
Longworth remarked, just a slob.
Now there was in the White House, as Wilson remarked, no
one in particular.)

His time is near. This, in the bitter air of a smudged morning, the little last crowd.

"No one has ever heard such cheers; I, who heard them in the streets of Paris, can never forget them in my life. I saw Foch pass, Clemenceau pass, Lloyd George, generals, returning troops, banners, but Wilson heard from his carriage something different, inhuman—or superhuman. Oh, the immovably shining, smiling man."

What is the true agony in S Street? What is the question? What had to be? What need not have been?

How can we know, more than the sliding leaves? How will it be seen in the overcast?

Was the hand moulding the world torn to pieces? Or did the hand falter? *Jornada del muerto.*

It will be seen that we worshiped false prophets and turned cool and blind in the heat-lightning of gods passing.

It will be seen perhaps that we recognized a god and moved hurriedly away.

It will be seen by subsequent generations ignorant too of their own times.

Wilson's voice is low slow but distinct:

"I am not one of those that have the least anxiety about the triumph of the principles I have stood for. I have seen fools resist Providence before and I have seen their destruction, as will come upon these again—utter destruction and contempt. That we shall prevail is as sure as that God reigns."

It will be seen . . .

FOR THE REASON OF
JUANA DE ASBAJE

. . . between a wretched and a happy lot,
not to the end that life may be preserved,
but to inflict a more protracted death.
—Juana de Asbaje (1651–1695);
trans. by Samuel Beckett

When I watch beyond iron fences
Nuns strolling in the toll of bells
Under the black, late-leafed locust trees,
I think of Sor Juana Inés de la Cruz—
Juana de Asbaje—
In Mexico three hundred years ago
Who lived as one of them for a brief life
Which may at the time have seemed long.
Poet, scientist, musician, Sor Juana
Had, it has been set down, great beauty,
Body and mind; one of which she denied.
I think of her
Because she was praised, but more
Because she was hated,
Because the Bishop of Puebla, tricked out in skirts,
Destroyed her; and two years after that
Sor Juana died nursing nuns in a plague.

Death? She knew several.
And the least was the last.

All this was not long
After the time of John Donne in England.
Could they have met, it would have been eye to eye,

As though a metaphysic wind had blown
West in those dolphin-diving sails
That bowing to the sun of afternoon
Seined the morning shining to farther thresholds.
Ashore in Mexico
After gun-thunder, hoof-thud, chain-smash,
The risen rites of talk,
Even the rustle of a book: the turning hand
Persistent as always.

So, I think, the silences of Sor Juana:
Soft in her nun's cell,
Cluster of robes round her walk,
Murmur and bead-click;
Risk of her pen—pause—risk again;
Bent over her compass at the world's shape;
Often, aubade and evensong,
Her far harp
Faint, strange down the corridors
Where, each alone, the curious sisters listened.

In San Miguel Nepantla
Nearby Amecameca
At the foot of Popocatepetl,
The Aztecs' old volcano,
Juana de Asbaje was born;
And once as a child, it was said,
In a passion of self-revenge
For her failure to learn cut all her hair away.
"Hair is not fair for a head so empty," she said.
And after—lovely again—
Her years as lady-in-waiting to the Vicereine
Did she remember that when cut for Christ?
Or only the lost man found in her poems?
"My love, my lord,
    hearken to my weary plaints awhile

as on the wind I cast them,"
She wrote, not meaning Christ; and said merely
To become a nun at eighteen
And despite her reservations in minor matters
"would,
in view of my refusal of marriage,
be fittest, least unbecoming."

Well—was it left to God?—she had
Two dozen years of work, her name in the world,
Until the Bishop of Puebla wrote the letter:
"Give it all up for faith in the Cross alone.
Signed: Sor Filotea."
And Sor Juana Inés de la Cruz—
Juana de Asbaje:
Fame, she replied, was sand beneath her feet,
But compass, books, pen, harp were hers
And any woman's anywhere.
The mind, having reasons, had its rights.

Did she bow in dusk through gardens?
I should like to see her so,
Treetops reddening in the last light,
Clutter of shadows on her robes,
Grave bending of her intelligent face.
No. There was wind over cactus
Until she stooped to the hot whips of sand
Lashing her eyes,
Until she could not bear
To be so envied for being so single.

It was then
She bowed in a way that queens might study
Into the darkened nunnery,
Stripped her cell of her professions
And signed her confession of faith with her own blood,

Denied her mind and died for truth.
Or what she said was truth
Or what the Bishop of Puebla said was truth.
For martyrs there are no questions, only answers,
And it is no matter.
It is only that the state of peace
Has to be bought and paid for.

So I think of Juana de Asbaje
In dusk, in the stroll of nuns through the bells,
Her beauty of body and mind,
Her brief life which has gone on so long
As to afflict her death.

THE TRANSITION

Went on then into a further country
Saw three white horses trotting down a green hill
To the bank of a river where willows were:
These in a steep shine of grass and water.

Things I had always known I saw there
For the first time; and things I had dreamed
As even now perhaps I dreamed while the horses
Bent to drink and I stood waiting for people.

Rain roved the land a moment and when the sun
Struck forth again there was a partial rainbow
Which I understood, and this was well enough
In uncertain pastures of indeterminate landscape.

Memoranda of leaves—do you remember?—
Were all I had to give you. As I waited
All those I seemed to gather back like mist
Until it became a body held in my arms.

NOTES

The One Door. There is a superstition among farmers, in New England at any rate, that generally you get a change of weather at the time of full moon. I believe recent scientific observation bears out the superstition as fact.

Lost Generation. Reference is to: Trumbull Stickney, George Cabot Lodge, David Graham Phillips, William Vaughn Moody, Frank Norris, Stephen Crane: a generation—our real lost generation—of American poets and novelists who all died young around the beginning of this century. In form, the poem imitates Emerson's *Hamatreya* and its dependent *Earth-Song.*

Peterborough. Reference is to Edwin Arlington Robinson and to a sonnet I wrote to him, as at Peterborough, when I was nineteen years old. Perhaps, this once in my life, it is not pointless to reprint a piece of juvenilia:

> When Time shall stalk contemptuous through this wood
> With none to see him or hear his feet
> Upon Monadnock's slope, or watch his hood
> Pass where the forests and the meadows meet,
> His stride will fade where fainter steps are lost,
> And through the pine trees a dark wind that grieves
> Will follow him like garments round a ghost,
> Stirring the lonely fall of the last leaves.
>
> Then in the utter silence of the night,
> Across the darkness of the ancient glen
> A cry of trumpets and a growing light
> Will herald the hoof-thuds of Arthur's men;
> And in among the trees abandoned here
> May flash the golden hair of Guinevere.

On Re-reading the Complete Works of an Elder Poet. Reference is to William Carlos Williams. I have dated the poem lest any reader think to see it as an obituary piece.

S Street. The prose passage about Wilson in Paris is from William Bolitho's *Twelve Against the Gods.*

For the Reason of Juana de Asbaje. I am completely indebted for my material to *An Anthology of Mexican Poetry,* translated by Samuel Beckett, compiled by Octavio Paz, preface by C. M. Bowra; (Indiana University Press, 1958).

W.T.S.

64